Become a Legendary Real Estate Agent
with a Legendary Mindset!

LIVING BERNIE'S MINDSET

DOLLY BAILEY

Real Estate Coach, Manager & Speaker

LIVING BERNIE'S MINDSET

DOLLY BAILEY

Become Your Own Star Publishing

Copyright © 2023 Dolly Bailey

The author of this Book does not dispense medical advice or prescribe the use of any technique as a form of treatment for physical, emotional, or medical problems without the advice of a physician, either directly or indirectly. The author's intent is only to offer information of a general nature to help you in your journey for emotional, physical, and spiritual well-being. If you use any information in this Book for yourself, the author and publisher assume no responsibility for your actions.

First edition

Imprint: Independently published
ISBN - 9798861451208

TABLE OF CONTENTS

This Book is dedicated to my Dad, Bernie.

I learned so much from him about how to treat people with respect and compassion. I learned work ethic at an early age, the joy of feeling pride in caring for all we had while having fun.

I will never forget your loving smile and calm wisdom.

Love you, Dad.

INTRODUCTION

Your Legacy is waiting on you.

If you are reading this Book right now, you've questioned yourself at some point, wondering why you're involved in this business. You're familiar with the stresses of real estate transactions and demanding clients who sometimes have unrealistic expectations.

On top of that, there's the constant worry that if a transaction falls through, you won't get paid.

You may also struggle with your health and weight, feeling defeated, depressed, sluggish, unattractive, and lacking confidence. It's completely normal to experience this range of emotions and frustrations as a thriving human being.

Are you ready to cultivate a winning mindset to help you create your desired Legacy?

The good news is that this book provides tips on developing a mindset that will make your career more enjoyable, improve your personal Life, and foster fulfilling relationships. Now is the time to make the decision. A decision that will put you on the path of moment-to-moment choices that shape you in the direction you want as opposed to where you don't want to be.

Throughout these pages, I will share the Mindset I learned from my Dad, Bernie. There are some things you learn from books, and then there are some things to learn from people who embody every trait. Bernie's Mindset is born from everything I learned from watching my father daily. While writing this Book, I have been interviewing family and friends. What a wonderful experience to realize that everyone around me also had this experience with him; I just never realized it! It is possible to be happy, work hard towards your goals, and create great success in the process. It starts with your Mindset and, without question, your willingness to participate. I am proud to share my collection of things I learned from my Dad and be a Real Estate manager living these ideas daily.

There are two types of people who will read this Book. The first type will search for reasons why it won't work for them, make excuses, and argue against the facts presented in this Book. The second type is open-minded, willing to consider new ideas, and respecting the proven practices that lead to a more positive mindset. Which type are you? The choice is yours and yours alone.

When my coach Kim Johnson asked me, "Where did you get your mindset" It all started with my Dad.

Growing up with a wonderful Mom and Dad who were married 45 years before they passed away, our family consisted of a loving older brother and sister, and then my parents had a surprise pregnancy 11 years later with twins! So, I have a wonderful twin brother. My parents had lived on a farm, which they sold but saved land across the road to build the house where I grew up in.

Eventually, my brothers and sister had homes on lots next to our parent's property. My Dad passed away when I was 28, and my Mom died when I was 29. My sweet sister passed away a few years ago. The family has always been so important to me, creating memories with each other. "Aunt Dolly" is always taking pictures to relish our experiences.   My loving husband Terry, of 36 years, and I never had children but are blessed with over 21 nieces and nephews, which we adore.

I want to share the Bernie Mindset and how I incorporated the beliefs my Dad lived throughout his life into today's winning Mindset for Agents.

Chapter 1- The Bernie Mindset

Growing up, my Dad positively influenced me; everyone loved him and wanted to be near him. Dad worked at Sears and Roebuck department store for over 32 years selling lawn tractors, and coworkers knew him as "Big Hearted Bernie."

People say children learn from watching their parent's actions and how they handle situations; my Dad had a gift! He always saw the good in everyone and everything.

I remember, as a child, someone came to visit our home, we had a long driveway leading up to our home, and right of way, as he was driving up, I felt myself already judging him. He had a car that needed a lot of work. When he exited the vehicle smiling, all my Dad saw was good in him. I remember that day like it was yesterday. It had a significant impact on me. As others around me were in judgment mode on this person, Dad could only see the good. I remember how much better that felt to look at things that way. The visitor could also feel my Dad's appreciation and genuine interest in them; this was the start of being conscious of my Mindset.

As Realtors, you have a new client on the phone, and are you making judgments about them based on their voice? Or a new client may walk in to meet you, and based on how they are dressed, you have a perceived notion about them. We all do this to some degree, and we are human. But does being judgmental attitude serve you as you are trying to be the best you can be? You never know what someone else might be going through in Life. Be kind.

I remember a story Dad told about buying a new truck with cash. Dad was working on the farm all day, and his truck broke down, so he drove to the local Ford dealer with cash to buy a new one. He had not changed clothes, so he probably smelled like the farm and looked like a farmer when he walked into the showroom at the dealership. Now, knowing my Dad, Bernie probably did not change his clothes as an experiment to see who was willing to help him (since Dad was a salesman himself). As the story goes, the first salesman kept walking when Dad walked in, but then another salesman came over and treated Dad as if he came into the showroom in a suit. That salesman sold a truck that day! When Dad returned to pick up the truck, he was dressed for work in his shirt and tie and loved that the salesperson who had just walked by him the day before was there to see him!   The salesman who did not judge Dad came with a mindset of service and was rewarded with future business from Dad all because the salesman had an attitude of service, not judgment.

In this story, which salesperson are you?

I think back to what my Dad did to cultivate this positive Mindset. Let's face it, he was in sales, too, with commissions based on how many lawn tractors he sold. Winter months were a little rough. There were ups and downs, just like all sales.

Bernie Loved his Garden.

Being outside in the garden and enjoying the fresh air and sunshine was Dad's meditation time and stress reliever. We did not have the typical garden size. It was huge, and he called it the truck patch. He would spend the morning in the garden before it got too hot outside, weeding, watering, and plowing to ensure healthy crops.

The garden and the vegetables it produced were very rewarding for Dad. It was a family affair to plant all the corn, potatoes, string beans, peas, beets, onions, tomatoes, melons, and more. The grandchildren (my nieces and nephews) would ride their minibikes to our house, and everyone would work together in the garden. When the family finished in the garden, we were tired and dirty but felt accomplished because we knew we would soon be enjoying our harvest, not to mention the quality time laughing and working together as a team effort.

Like prospecting for business as Agents, it takes time to plant the seeds and get your name out there in the community to show your value and how you can help the consumers. In time you will reap the rewards of your prospecting and planting seeds. The daily activities are what bring the results/harvest. Prospecting is more than instant gratification; just like the garden needs time to grow, so does your business. The garden needs rain, weeding, and nurturing for a bountiful harvest. As you take the time to promote your relationships and business and take care of your clients, you will feel accomplished at the end of the day, knowing you added value to someone, and that is a big part of your building a winning mindset.

Bernie had a passion for his vehicles.

The next thing I would hear in the morning was Dad washing his truck. Dad always had to make his truck shiny and clean to go to work. Clean vehicles made him feel proud driving his sharp-looking truck. He always wanted us to care for our things; our parents worked very hard to buy things, so caring for them was important. When my brother and I were young, we sometimes washed our bikes as Dad washed his truck. We were so proud of our cool bikes.

As Realtors, do you notice how much better you feel when your car is washed and cleaned on the inside? I always said my car ran faster when it was clean! When you show up for an appointment with a clean car, that says a lot about you to your clients too. They think you found them important enough to show up with a clean vehicle and look professional.

All these little things set the tone for your day and a positive Mindset.

Do you have a clean car
and clutter-free interior?

Awareness

Dad believed in setting goals. The first thing is to know where you are in Life and what improvements are wanted.

Rate yourself 1 - 10 in the following categories of Life.

1 being dissatisfied - 10 being you are thrilled with where you are.

______ **Health and fitness**

______**Mental state/ clarity**

______**Emotional state/happy**

______**Spiritual/Connection to source**

______**Career/Profession**

______**Finances**

______**Spouse or significant other relationship**

______**Family//children relationships**

______**Fun time**

Use this space to take your notes:

Note where your levels of satisfaction fall. Once you have chosen the areas you want to work on, it is time to get laser focused.

For example, If your Health is an area, you would look to improve. Knowing things you need to do differently to get better results is essential.

You will also notice old patterns of how you act when triggered, which you need to adjust to continue progressing. For example, you had a terrible day, one of your real estate closings fell apart, and on your way home from work, you want to stop for a drink or maybe get ice cream, something the old you would do. Being conscious is where you are aware of your feelings and break the pattern! Awareness is so essential to making the small shifts to become the best version of you possible! Instead, a nice cool iced tea with lemon might do the trick, or go for a walk and shift your focus.

Have you ever had a gut feeling about a client and thought, I don't think I want to work with them, but you do anyway because you need the business, only to regret the decision? Now that you are more aware, you can make better decisions. You were aware that these clients needed to align with who is your ideal client, and you were not a match. Agents will also tell me these clients are wasting my time, but I have so much time and gas money invested in them I don't want to stop now. A scarcity mindset does not serve you. When you decide to cut loose those clients who are time wasters who don't listen to your advice, are demanding, and stress you out, you are now working from an abundance mindset. Now you are telling the universe I am free to work with other qualified clients, and I don't need to hang on to a client that is not serious about buying a house. One of my agents had this exact experience, she was very reluctant to cut her clients loose because of the time she had invested in them to this point, but she did it anyway, and the same day got two other lead calls out of nowhere.

 Please figure out what your ideal client looks like, how you will feel when working with them, whether they respect your guidance and knowledge, their hobbies, where they shop, what cars they drive, etc. Now you know your ideal client and get to attract those types of clients through your targeted marketing and your positive focus on who can benefit from you as a real estate professional. Make Real Estate more fun by working with the clients you choose to serve.

What does your ideal client look like?

Use this space to take your notes:

Knowing what you want and why-

Sometimes people need help with what it is they want. If you don't know what you want, then who does? Without absolute Clarity of what you want, Life will seem random, and you will get what Life throws at you. OR.... Do you know what you want, but your limiting beliefs tell you it is Not Possible? Fears stop you from acknowledging what you want. Fears of rejection, heartbreak, I am not good enough, will create confusion in our minds. Logic will get us from point A to B.

> "Imagination will take you Everywhere, with Imagination nothing is impossible"
>
> - Albert Einstein

Be courageous to claim what it is you want...Clarity is the key.

Once I have an idea of what I want to accomplish, sometimes to concrete the concept for me, I will make a Pro's and Con's list of what will happen and how I will feel once I hit my goal and then a cons list of what will happen if I don't hit my goal or how it will make me feel. Examples: I want to do 10% more volume in my real estate business next year. Pros are what I can do with that extra money, but Con's are I feel they will need to take even more time away from family. Then I can work with the agents on freeing up time with an assistant and a transaction coordinator and take advantage of the systems their Broker offers that they need to utilize. Plus, evaluate how they spend their time during the day and how much is on lead-generating activities or busy work. Another example; I want to lose 30 pounds—Pros of how good I will feel, increased energy, looking good in clothes. Cons If I don't lose weight, I will have deteriorating Health, my joints will continue to get worse, and I will have low self-esteem and a lack of confidence.

It is deciding what you want and why with Clarity is essential.

 You need to know What you want and focus on something other than the How.

"Nothing is Impossible, the word itself says I'm Possible"

- Audrey Hepburn

Make sure your dream of what you want is yours and not someone else's. Don't be afraid to dream big. This is where I hear my Dad saying, " If you want something, go for it, kid. You can do whatever you set your mind to do".

What do you want?

How will you feel when you have accomplished this?

When my coach mentioned I should write a book with all my real estate experiences of 36 years and working hands-on with so many agents and knowing their daily challenges and how I help them with their mindsets so they can go on to be successful personally and professionally, I said NO WAY.

She told me you love coaching agents; you can become a coach and have people pay for your coaching. I said I could not write a book. Plus, I was afraid agents would not want to pay me for coaching.

Who am I? I never had a degree to coach, and I am not a psychologist. I felt physically sick every time the subject came up—massive fear of failure and judgment from what others would think. I got stuck in the HOW. How do I begin writing a book or going about a coaching business? I hear voices saying, "Who do you think you are to try this; I am 60 years old. I could go on and on with excuses and get hung up in HOW and FEAR.

My coach reels me back in and gets me to focus on what I want first. What I wanted was to be able to help agents both personally and professionally. I get so much joy from knowing that I helped someone through a problem or helped them see their value and set up a plan to reach their goals.

My coach reeled me back off the ledge. Once I knew what I wanted, we could plan strategies and get to the how step by step. A coach is so important; they see things in you that it is hard to see yourself, and coaches help guide you to what it is you want in Life and call you out on your excuses.

So many times, in goal setting with the agents, they will be afraid to put their goal too high because they don't want to be disappointed if they don't hit the goal. So, they want to set something they can reach. Know what goal would excite you. What will you do with your money? A trip, a new house, a new car, jewelry, take a missionary trip. Your goal should have excitement attached to it. If you knew you couldn't fail, what would your goal be? Get excited about your goal.

Once you have your goal, visualize it daily, write affirmations, and create a vision board of your house, cars, trips, whatever it is for you. Be specific about how you feel when your goal becomes a reality.

What do you TRULY WANT?

How will you feel when you have it?

Are you feeling that way now?

Make a Decision-

Once you have decided what you want to be or have, it is liberating. Please be honest with yourself. Are you 100% committed to your decision?   It becomes much easier because it is now non -negotiable. Once a decision becomes a plan, it brings Clarity to your mind. You start to put yourself in situations for success. For example, if you are trying to stop drinking and be sober, you will stop going to bars or parties where the focus is on drinking. You will find other interests and friends who enjoy activities that align with who you are becoming. If you have decided to lose 30 pounds to become leaner and healthier, you find yourself being strong to choices that no longer serve the new you. If you want to raise your Real Estate Sales by 10%, you will make the extra calls and activities needed to succeed. If you have decided to take the family on a Disney trip this year and told the kids, there is no turning back!

Fear is Real. A trap that keeps us from making decisions and taking action - fear of the unknown, fear of failure, fear of being judged, fear of rejection, and even fear of success for some. Face your fears as if it is impossible to fail. Besides, what is the worst thing that could happen if you fail? Then ask yourself what is the best thing to happen if you succeed! Does the best possible scenario outweigh the worst possible scenario? I remember when I was only in the business a few years ago, having lunch with my Broker and sharing my dream of having a condo oceanfront in Ocean City, Md. She said, "Well, let's go," and look at several condos. Of course, immediately, the fear set in, and I started all the excuses. She said, "What is the worst-case scenario?" You can sell it if it doesn't work out. We took off that afternoon and drove to the beach, met a Realtor, and looked at a few condos in my limited price range (because it had to be oceanfront). The process of looking at these condos was so fun and exciting. I selected one, and I called my husband and told him what I was thinking. He said ok. He joined me that weekend to look at the one I selected, and we bought our first beach place. Two things I want to point out in this story: feel free to share your dream with other like-minded people. Plus, I would have NEVER bought a beach property without the encouragement of my Broker and helping me remove my fears. Having supportive and positive people around you is a game changer. My Dad and Mom were so proud of us for fulfilling our dream. Dad

always favored taking a leap of faith as long as we were
on the adventure together.

> " Someone somewhere is depending on you to do the thing you were called to do."

Agents needing more confidence or have low self-esteem come up with excuses to avoid taking the first action step towards their goal. They are also good at sabotaging themselves. Some agents don't believe they deserve to be successful because of past traumas or life experiences. Working with agents who struggle with a lack of confidence starts with celebrating small wins. They drank eight glasses of water every day for a week. They stopped by a For Sale By Owner (FSBO). They called one expired listing. They took a class to gain more real estate knowledge. One agent I noticed was awkward when they smiled, and it was because they didn't like how their teeth looked.

I find many agents who lack confidence and don't like how they look in their clothes, weight loss is essential for them. When I received an invitation to speak in front of our real estate company's kickoff event, where 210 agents were in attendance many years ago—It was to be a motivational speech for 30 minutes. My Immediate response was NO WAY. First, I had a fear of public speaking. Visions of me as a kid in church practicing for the Christmas play where I had to sing Hark the Herald Angels Sing in front of everyone and almost passed out, yes I had to sit down with my head between my knees. Thank goodness this was just during practice. With lots of practice, I pulled off the Christmas show just fine.

My second thought was, I don't want to be embarrassed walking on stage holding onto handrails with my bad knees; gosh, I hope there are handrails; what will I wear so I don't look fat? Fear of the unknown was spinning in my head. I just kept saying No. Finally, I agreed to take on the challenge. If I ask my agents to get outside their comfort zone daily, I need to. So, I began practicing every morning for 30 minutes for the month before the event. Somewhere I read that if you practice your speech repeatedly, even if you draw a blank when you get in front of everyone, hopefully, out of repetition, your speech will just come to you. The speech was successful; I didn't pass out and got a standing ovation! Again, I must thank my previous boss for pushing me beyond my comfort zone. So when you have somebody in your corner who believes in you and is pushing you to expand yourself, don't let fear rob you of the joy you can experience and what you can do for others.

If you want to be a top real estate agent and have a positive mindset, you must monitor the messages coming into your mind so they are in harmony with the Life you want to live. Consider the TV you watch, the books you read, and the people you associate with. Do they drag you down or support your vision?

I have a Morning Mindset group that meets every other week for 30 minutes. We share wins and ask for help with challenges we might be experiencing, but more importantly, we support each other with tips on getting our mornings started with a solid positive mindset to conquer the day.

The morning routine is essential to set the stage for how the rest of the day will go. Are you intentional with meditation, affirmations, visualization, exercise, reading, and journaling?

Hal Elrod, author of The Miracle Morning for Realtors, says even 5 minutes in the morning will help your Mindset for the days you are short on time.

Do you have a positive morning routine?

What do you want to incorporate into your morning routine?

What would make your day outstanding?

Use this space to take your notes:

Agents experiencing burnout or have excuses of I'm too young; I'm too old, I need more confidence, can benefit from Clarity of their goal or dream and then practice an intentional morning routine talking about their vision, visualizing, and feeling it! Example: If buying a beach house is your dream, imagine the ocean, smell the salt air, feel the sand between your toes walking the beach, and hear your family enjoying themselves at your beach home.

Bernie Dressing for a Successful Day

When Dad would leave the house for work, he always was dressed for a good sales day, with a shirt and tie, and smelled good, I can never forget his cologne, and he gave kisses to everyone and out the door to step into his clean, shiny truck with a big smile beaming with pride! Down the driveway, he would go waving through the window.

How are you dressing for success today? When you dress in business attire, do you notice that you feel more like a successful salesperson? Some people need to put on specific shoes, even if they are working from home, so they feel like they are now in work mode. During covid, when everyone was at home, the suggestions were to get up, shower, get dressed in something other than your jammies, as well as put on a splash of perfume or cologne "as if" you were going to work. All these things tell your mind you are now in work mode. When you look good, you feel good. You give off positive energy to attract positive experiences when you feel good.

I hear so often today how Realtors are showing up at showings of properties dressed in gym attire or shorts and tee shirts with baseball caps. Just know that the ring cameras are watching, the neighbors are observing, and they are astonished at how what we call "Professional

Realtors " are showing up. I have had situations where calls came in from a seller who saw on the ring camera what appeared to be someone trying to break into their home. It ended up being the Realtor trying to find the lockbox to get it for a showing. The Realtor was in a baseball hat and gym clothes. Do these poor buyers have a chance of getting their offer accepted working with a Realtor like this, especially in a multiple-contract market? Remember, your dress affects your clients and everyone else watching you. But more importantly, your Mindset. Set yourself up for success. Dress like how you want to be perceived.

I heard an extremely successful Realtor say she noticed as she started to dress a little more casually with her repeat customers, who were now friends, and her referrals stopped. Her friends continued to use her but stopped referring her to others. I found that very interesting. Be referable. Take the extra step of dressing for the referral business. Your friends want to refer you and want you to make them feel proud when you meet their referral for the first time.

If you show up dressed for success and with a positive Mindset, ready to serve, watch out!

Summary of Bernie's Mindset

*Do you find yourself judging others?

*What daily activities are you doing to nurture your business?

*Is your car clean?

*What is your one area of Life to work on?

*What do you want? Dream Big.

*Why do you want it?

*Who is your ideal client?

*What is one activity that you can do consistently to move you closer to your goal?

*What does your morning routine look like to set you up for success?

*How will your day be different living in the Bernie mindset?

Being aware of these things and taking action will cultivate a winning mindset!

Use this space to take your notes:

Chapter 2 --Health and Well-being

This topic is such a tricky one for most of us and I am no exception to the topic.

Dad was a smoker most of his life and died at 63 of lung cancer. His exercise was working in the garden or the garage. He loved his beer on his days off and after he got home from work as a nightcap. He would rub his beer belly and say it was all paid for! Diet and exercise were never a conscious focus of our family. Our meals included meat, mashed potatoes, gravy, and corn from the garden.

I was always chunky as a kid, even though my twin brother was very thin.

In those days, Mom would order my school clothes from the Sears catalog. I was "chubby" size. Amazing how that was a politically correct size back then. I have struggled with my weight all my Life. I have gained and lost more weight than I care to think about. My Mom died 11 months after Dad with a massive heart attack at the age of 64; her death certificate said the cause of death was obesity. Sometimes I think being chubby runs in my family; I should admit this is my body. Food was a celebration when something good happened when there was sadness when you were bored while watching TV. I was an emotional eater. As a teenager I was on a diet after diet.

As my career in real estate grew, so did my waistline.
The crazy hours and stressful days fueled by fast
food stops on the road and emotional eating.
I told myself I deserved to eat what I wanted because I
had worked so hard that day. It didn't take long until the
extra weight took a toll on my knees and mojo.

Being self-conscious of how you look in your
clothes affects your confidence personally and
professionally. Meeting clients for the first time,
showing them property where you walk up
steps totally out of breath. Going to networking
events because you know that will help your
business but dread meeting people looking like
you do. Shopping for business clothes once you can
no longer fit in the regular stores' sizes is very
depressing. Plus, the styles could be more attractive.

How about the business lunch, and you get to the
restaurant where they want to sit at a booth and
know you will not fit in? I understand the toll that being
out of shape and overweight has on your Mindset.
You don't understand why you have so much
trouble losing weight. You are feeling down, which
causes you to go for comfort food. Your energy level
is at an all-time low. It is a downward spiral.

Now having said that, I always had a happy face while
with my agents or at meetings and events because I
did like all those things but found myself
exhausted at the end of the day, and my knees hurting
and disgusted with my overall condition and
limitations.

My previous Broker and dear friend came to have a
heart-to-heart talk with my husband and me about my
weight condition, and she didn't want to see me die
early from a heart attack. Of course, neither did I.
The discussion was on considering gastric bypass
surgery. I did not want to hear about it. That surgery
just seemed so drastic.   More time went by of low
energy, unsuccessful weight loss, hurting knees,
sleep apnea, and daily disappointments.

My husband has always supported me in whatever I
wanted to do and loved me unconditionally, no matter
my size. It was coming to the point where I thought I
would see what was involved with the surgery and
the cost since our insurance did not cover gastric
bypass surgery. After long thought and consideration.
We decided we were going to go for it. In October of
2014 I had the surgery, and things went well. The weight
kept coming off for the first year and a half after surgery.

Once my stomach healed and I could eat more variety of
foods, it came to watching what I ate just like before
surgery. The only difference was that I could not eat as
much at a time.

But your eating habits and triggers were still there.
That is why some people gain all their weight back.
Their Mindset on food had stayed the same. I am going
on year nine since surgery and have gained some
weight back, but I am working on getting that weight
back off. I had both knees replaced in the last
Twelve months so I am ready to move around
with ease!

I know as well as anyone the mental battle that goes
on within us when we do not feel like ourselves and
weight is a problem.

Agents tell me I need to do videos, but I want
to wait until I lose 20 pounds.   I don't like how I look.
You hide from pictures taken. The agents tell
me about the depression and inability to get
back on track with their real estate career; a lot of it is how
they see themselves.
They are embarrassed about their weight gain and don't
like how they look, so they stop prospecting and doing
activities they know will bring them success.

This extra weight you carry stops you from living the life you deserve.

Your commitment to health, fitness, and weight loss is a determination and self-love mindset.

Depression is something agents deal with, whether it is from lack of money coming in, kids having trouble in school, alcoholism, the death of a loved one, or being a caretaker for elderly parents suffering from migraines. Everyone struggles with something within their families. Find a way to get more sleep, exercise, and eat healthier to keep yourself strong.

Big-Hearted Bernie's Legacy lives on through his children and grandchildren. We all learned how to love, have fun, and connect over a work project, gardening, or working in the garage. How to have pride, believe in people, and see the good in them. Make people feel special with your actions and comments.

Work hard and play hard. Life is short!

Summary of Health and Well being

*Is your Health or physical condition getting in the way of your success?

*In what way is your Health or physical condition getting in your way?

*What needs to change?

*What is one activity or activities that you should do consistently to move you toward a healthier lifestyle?

*Who will be your accountability partner?

*How will your Life be different once you reach your goal?

Use this space to take your notes:

Chapter 3 - Dealing with Stress

Stress affects everyone a little differently. Some people, when stressed, Smoke, Drink, Eat, Do Drugs, Exercise, Shop, and spend money. Stress is very real in how it affects your Health. Everyone has stress; it just comes down to how we deal with and defuse it. Do things that make you happy: a round of golf, a massage, listening to your favorite music, walking in the sunshine, meditating, or running.

Being a Realtor is a very stressful career. You are dealing with people experiencing a lot of stress in their lives. They are moving because of death, divorce, health issues, and foreclosure on their home; they can no longer handle the home they raised their family in for years and must go into nursing homes. Just the fact that you recognize the fact that your client is suffering from the stress of the situation will help you be the rock and leader they need right now. When dealing with unrealistic clients, agents say this client is sucking the Life out of me. Over time this takes a toll on you if you need to take care of yourself. The old saying is, "You have to take care of yourself so you can be there and care for others." Keeping hydrated and eating healthier (have healthy snacks and water in your car) will prevent you from driving through fast-food restaurants. After the call from an upset client, take a short walk, get some fresh air, and breathe. Don't take things so personally. Try to let the negativity roll off of you.

Some simple stress relievers are decluttering your home office, junk drawer, closet, and car. If you have been walking past an area in your house that has been driving you crazy, it is time to clean it up, and you will feel so good and accomplished when everything is clean. All these little things add up to preserving you and stabilizing your stress levels.

Giving always makes you feel good too. After a big snowstorm, Dad would love to take the big allis chalmers tractor to plow the back road and neighboring properties. He loved giving and helping others. Find ways for you to gift or help others less fortunate than yourself.

Overwhelmed is something I hear a lot. Agents say, "There are so many things to do," the overwhelm paralyzes the agents from getting anything done. Or maybe your house is a train wreck because you have been working long hours and have not had time to clean up; the laundry is stacked up, dishes are in the sink, and the garage is so full you can't even get your car inside anymore. When facing overwhelmed, pick the most critical item that needs to be conquered first. Conquer that one, then select the next one.

Have you ever suffered from a state of overwhelm that just paralyzed you from progress?

You are not alone.

Stress from the long hours working weekends and holidays away from family and special events. It is challenging when the spouse or children do not understand why you must work instead of being with them. Even at home, you are on your computer and phone working and not present with them.

How do you handle these conversations and expectations with family?

In the past, I had agents sit with their children and explain that If I can make _____ more sales, I will get you that new bike, or we will go to the beach for the weekend. Then the family has more buy-in as to why you are working so hard to be able to buy them a bike! The children might even push you out the door to go to work!

The unpredictable paychecks cause a lot of stress. The Real Estate business has its ups and downs, and when times are good, you spend everything you make and sometimes forget to save for a rainy day, which causes a lot of anxiety in slow times. Setting up a financial plan to take money out of your commission check before you get the cash in your hands is helpful, saving some money for your income taxes. Your clients can feel it when you need the sale more than they need the house. Your desperation shows.

My Dad always taught us about saving money and spending wisely. My Mom always said it is not what you make but what you save. She was a very hard worker and worked in a sewing factory, pressing and steaming clothes while standing all day.   I grew up in an environment where you saved money until you could buy it; if you needed a loan for something, it was small. Credit cards back then were for emergencies only.

Do you have a financial planner set up to help you with your savings plan?

When you have client parties or farming neighborhoods, do you have any sponsors to help with your expenses? You can help promote their business as they help you with costs.

More agents are getting full-time jobs and trying to work Real Estate part-time. That is very stressful because to serve our clients, we need to be available when they are to look at properties and attend inspections and closings. This puts a lot of stress on Agents because they are trying to juggle everything and always feel they are leaving someone down, people at work, family at home, or clients.

For agents who are parents, having reliable, short-notice child care coverage is so important so they can make appointments with clients. Client appointments also stress families more to accommodate the flexible schedule agents have to work around.

Go to the Office to Work. Some people need to be more focused at home and truly focus on client calls and lead generation without barking dogs in the background and loud children. You miss the synergy of the office and connecting with the other agents when you work from home. Organizing your workspace saves so much time. When you need something, you know right where to find it. Plus, having clutter-free workspace frees the mind to focus on what matters.

Where do you work best, from the office or home?

An Accountability Partner or Coach can help with your stress level by having someone to bounce ideas off of and discuss things that work for them or challenges you are experiencing. Plus, with your diet and fitness plan, an accountability partner to keep you on track is super helpful!

Summary of Stress and How to relieve it.

What are things that cause you the most stress professionally?

What are things that cause you the most stress personally?

What are some things that you can do to relieve some stress?

Do you find yourself taking everything too personally?

Do you feel overwhelmed?

What one thing can you do to reduce your state of overwhelm?

Do you find yourself when giving to others that you feel amazing?

Does your family know the expectations of being a successful agent and what that means to them?

Where do you work best, in the office or at home?

Being surrounded by other like-minded people who support you will raise you. Who is someone you need to reach out to for more support?

Use this space to take your notes:

59

Chapter 4- Bernie's Way of Time Management

Dad got up early and loved to get started working outside in the morning. Growing up as teenagers, my brother and I would like to sleep in a little later on weekends. Well, if we were still in bed by 9:00 am. We would either hear, "Don't let the sun burn a hole in your butt," or Dad would drive the tractor outside our bedroom windows to wake us up. Dad knew if we got up and finished all our work, we could do fun things later in the day.   The drive-in movies in the convertible with a cooler and snacks or going to the Carnivals only happened once we finished the work. We knew the expectations for the day.

As Agents, are you disciplined enough to get your lead generation done early in the day? We all know that our days can run away quickly with showings and last-minute details in our real estate transactions. Then if there is time left in the day, we try to have family or some personal time. It feels like the day runs us instead of us running our days.

Just think if you time blocked the morning for lead generation, time for personal things, time blocked loved ones' special dinner dates or soccer practice. You could structure your day with intention and accomplish much more, and your family will be much happier too. Have fun during family time guilt-free. But then work with focus during lead generation time. Work Hard, Play Hard!

A lot of my agent's time blocks first thing in the morning to do their meditation, gratitude journaling, exercising, and writing their affirmations before they even think about anything else. Champions set up their Mindset to have the best day ever! Getting up a little earlier to fit in some extra activities before your day gets too busy is worth it. You will feel so much more prepared and focused for your day. You feel proactive instead of reactive to your day.

Are you letting your day run you, or are you intentionally setting yourself up for success?

Dad was very good at getting things done and sharing with everyone what we would be working on around the house, so we all knew the expectations. We had a huge garden, so summers were hectic in the garden or helping Dad with projects in the garage. There was no TV time during the day, and there was work and fresh air outside. We only realized how special the talks with Dad were while working on projects once we got older. This time spent was invaluable for Dad to know what was happening in our lives, and we felt special hanging out with him. Even the grandchildren that lived next door would ride their minibikes up to our house to hang out with Dad and work on cars and lawn tractors and help in the garden because we were all allowed to make mistakes and make messes, and we were imperfectly perfect in Dad's eyes. I grew up with the "Done is Better than Perfect." When we were all done for the day, we were tired but very proud of all our accomplishments.

If you long for more quality time with family members or your spouse, plan it like an appointment! Have date nights, game nights with kids, Sunday Church, or whatever is special for you.

It is time to time block your schedule with the non-negotiable activities you need to complete to become the best version of yourself. I hear constantly; well, I don't have time for ____.   Then you don't want it bad enough, period. Whether it is exercise, taking a class, joining a networking group, or making lead-generating calls. Get up earlier, start with 15 minutes, to gain extra time to get in the non-negotiables. Planning the night before, make sure you fill the car with gas, have your healthy snacks and lunch packed, bottles of water, have your workout clothes by your bed, and be ready to do your Morning Routine! Some of my agents love making a list of things to do for the next day. It helps them sleep, knowing they are ready to go when they wake up. There is something that feels so good to cross items off your "to-do" list! Sometimes I will add things to my list that I just got done so I have the pleasure of crossing off.

Delegate work that others can do. Take advantage of Transaction coordinators or systems your real estate company offers to help with lead generation, databases, and social media posting.

There needs to be more than great intentions; you must follow through with the activities. People are great at planning, buying new sneakers for exercising, purchasing exercise equipment, getting a new water bottle to help them drink more water, and purchasing a new journal so they can write their gratitude every day. They prepare a list of all the prospects they want to call but never take action or only do it a couple of times.

You have already decided what you want; now it is time to take action and make it happen. The activities getting done separates the successful Realtors from those who are not. As Realtors, your days can change quickly with showings, clients wanting to write contracts, and issues needing your attention. Time Block the non-negotiable activities early in your day for best results.

Procrastination is something that a lot of people suffer from, especially the perfectionist. Because they want to make sure everything is perfect before they move forward.

If the perfectionist is creating a marketing flier to send out, they end up fooling with the flier for hours to make sure it is just right, and sometimes, the flier never gets sent out because it is not perfect, or now the flier is no longer relevant.

If you were in my office, you would have heard me say, "Done is far better than perfect!" I have seen a lot of procrastination with doing videos. The agents know they need to do Videos, but typical excuses are, I don't have the right content to post, my hair doesn't look nice today, and I don't like how my voice sounds. Let's face it, people watching videos prefer authentic you anyway. We all want to look good when on camera, but letting it stop you from providing valuable information that can help your clients with their real estate journey is not helpful.

Don't let fear stop you from moving forward. Procrastination from starting a diet and fitness routine "I will start Monday Morning" Why not now?

Be careful of advice from friends and family who might mean well but tell you why you shouldn't move forward with your dream. Sometimes they are jealous because if you succeed, it will make them look bad for not moving forward; they will prefer you to stay with them in their comfort zone. Sometimes they don't want to see you hurt if it doesn't go as planned for you. I would reach out to people who are already successful in what you want to accomplish and take advice from them.

Watch your Self Talk. The most important person you have a conversation with is yourself. Pay attention to what you are telling yourself. Are you in a positive mindset? Repeating your affirmations and then visualizing your success. Are you your biggest fan? What do you say to yourself daily? Is it serving you, or is an adjustment needed? Awareness is the key to shifting your self-talk to Optimism and Confidence.

Staying Consistent with your personal goals and lead-generating activities is one of the most common challenges I hear. Clarifying what you want, scheduling your non-negotiable activities (time blocking), and your commitment to your goal is essential. Hiring an assistant or media manager to help you stay consistent with your actions might be an option.

How do you stay consistent with your personal goals?

How do you stay consistent with your professional goals?

Focus on the Activities, and the Results will come! In our immediate gratification world, I see Realtors who try something a few times and give up because they didn't see immediate Results. Prepare yourself for the journey as you become the best version of yourself personally and professionally.

Summary of Bernies Time Management

What time do you start your day?

In the morning, you will most likely get a jump start to your non-negotiable activities. What are your Non-negotiables every day?

When is your best time of day to block time for lead generation?

How do you best avoid procrastination?

Set your calendar with vacations, kid's events, and date nights like appointments. Family is everything. Enjoy this time guilt-free.   But what time is left, work intentionally and make the most of it.

Clarity of your goals will keep you motivated and energized to keep doing the activities necessary to be successful. All while having the Bernie Mindset!

Use this space to take your notes:

Chapter 5. The Art of Communicating

Dad was an excellent communicator because he was a good listener, calm, and present as you talked with him.

Communication in the Real Estate Industry is essential. The Realtors Association of York and Adams Counties said their number one issue that comes across the Grievance Committee's desk is the need for more communication. Today, texting and emailing instead of picking up the phone or talking face-to-face about whatever is happening has caused much tension and misunderstanding.

When you speak face- to- face you can see facial reactions and body language as to what is going on with your clients and their fears or hot buttons. I once was speaking to a couple that we just saw the perfect house for them. The wife was excited, and I thought the husband was on board. When we got to the office to write up the agreement of sale, I noticed the husband's body language was not engaged anymore. So, I started asking questions and realized the husband needed to feel comfortable with the payments and exactly how much money they needed before we could proceed. If I had been texting or emailing or just sent the offer electronically, I would not have been able to help the buyers with their concerns. I might have gotten an " I want to think about it" stall.

There are some agents who, when a problem arises, stick their heads in the sand and pretend it is not happening rather than deal with it. It is because they fear what the client will do or say. Some will text the client so they don't have to talk with them. Communicating is not hiding from clients. The sooner you can call or meet with your client to explain what is happening, the better. Understand that when you give the client terrible news, expect them to fear what this news means to them. Be there with options and compassion to help them.

How do you rank as a communicator? (on a scale of 1 to 10, 10 being the best.)

Do I express my ideas in a clear and understandable way?

Am I using jargon or technical terms that might confuse others?

Do I provide context or explanations when needed?

Am I genuinely listening to what others are saying, or am I just waiting to respond?

Do I ask follow-up questions to show that I'm engaged in the conversation?

Am I avoiding interrupting or finishing sentences for others?

What does my body language convey?

Am I maintaining eye contact and am I considering the feelings and perspectives of the other person?

Am I responding with empathy when they share their experiences?

Am I using a friendly and respectful tone?

> **The most important thing in communication is to hear what isn't being said.**
>
> **– Peter Drucker**

Use this space to take your notes:

Teamwork

Lately, agents have complained about other agents not communicating with them. With the market we are in right now, with multiple offers and very time-sensitive communications needed by everyone, the frustration is at an all-time high.

Let's follow the golden rule to treat others as you would like to be treated.

What you **don't** want done to you:

*When you write a contract for another agent, and they do not confirm with you that they received your offer or follow up with you when they meet the seller to present your offer. After the deadline had passed for the seller to respond to the offer, there still needed to be an update from the other agent. Meantime the buyers are calling you wanting to know what is happening.

*An agent emails you an offer on one of your listings late in the evening but doesn't text you to alert you there is an offer in your email, but they want their contract presented that same evening.

*Buyer agents sent incomplete contracts, missing proof of funds, or pre-approval letters.

*Demanding agents who are very aggressive or arrogant with you.

*No response from other agents when you text or call them.

*The seller wants to wait for days to collect several offers before they look at the offer you presented to the listing agent the first day the home was for sale.

*Other people need to pick up the phone to talk.   They only want to text or email.

*Being accused of unethical behavior if your buyer's contract was the one the seller chose to work with.

*Agents go on vacation and don't tell anyone because they don't want to give up any commission to have another agent to help them, or they believe they can do it all themselves from their computer and phone. But they are very slow to respond to calls, texts, and emails.

To have better teamwork with your fellow agents, talk with each other and set expectations and timelines so everyone knows the rules. Be the agent that everyone wants to work with. Your reputation matters. Your behavior has consequences.

When do we text, email, call, or meet face-to-face in communications?

What type of communication is acceptable when writing up contracts?

When is texting considered an acceptable form of communication?

When negotiating a contract, what type of communication is acceptable?

How do you leave people feeling after you communicate with them?

Use this space to take your notes:

Gut check on the first impression you leave on people. When they walk away, are they thinking, "I will never use them again," or do they feel like you are the agent they want to continue working with? How did you make them feel?

Like eating in a restaurant and you don't like your meal, the waitress says, "How is everything, good?" We answer yes. But when we leave the restaurant, we say we don't have to go back there again. According to the waitress, we answered that everything was good, and that was all she knew. We didn't want to hurt anyone's feelings. So you need to understand that people are only sometimes 100% honest. People don't tell you what they are thinking to your face.   It is essential to have them feel comfortable enough to share their thoughts with you. Asking good questions is vital to learn about them and their needs. The more they know you care about them and their needs, the more teamwork and referrals will happen for you.

Bernie Being Present at the moment.

Dad would drink coffee, chat with Mom in the morning about their day, and talk with us kids as we ran around getting ready for our days. He made a point to be present for Mom and us if we stopped long enough to chat! Dad was excellent at being present with anyone who was with him. You knew he was listening to you. You felt cared for and that he was interested in You.

Do you find yourself being present with loved ones? There are so many distractions today with all the electronics. Make your time with loved ones count so they feel heard; 15 minutes is better than 2 hours of everyone on their phones in the same room.   I am so guilty of this. As Realtors, when your phone rings, you answer it; your loved one might have been mid-sentence, and you drop them like a hot potato to answer the call. It takes effort to make time for the people that matter the most. You can schedule date nights to ensure quality time with your family and friends. Take an exercise or painting class together, and work on a project together. Knowing that you are connecting with your loved ones feels fantastic.

When Dad and Mom bought the farm at auction, Dad was also going to buy some of the farm equipment. So he asked my older brother, a youngster then, to sit on the different tractors to see which one he could best reach the tractor pedals, which would be the tractor that Dad would buy. My brother felt special because Dad wanted his input to purchase the tractor so he could help Dad on the farm.

I just learned about a story where one of the grandkids rode his bike to visit Mom and Dad. Some family issues were going on at the time, and my Dad calmly sat down for an hour and explained to an 8-year-old how others can interpret your actions differently and the great importance of family. The grandson felt like Dad understood what he was going through, and the conversation greatly impacted him that day. The grandson went on to do a school project on my Dad and referred to him as an owl, Wise, and Calm.

When it comes to your real estate business, are you a good listener? Are you listening to your client's needs and wants or just waiting so you can talk, or worse yet, cutting them off or talking over them? If you cut your client off while they are talking, you are showing them what they are saying is less important than what you are saying. One thing I learned from Dad was listening to and asking questions with a curious mind. Be knowledgeable so you can be the best resource possible for the client. Dad shared with me that a new salesperson had started working with him at Sears, and he was so impressed because she took the manual for one of the push mowers home and tore apart her mower so she understood everything about the mower so she could best sell the product. When I started my first job at a golf course at 15 years old, almost 16 years old, part of my job was selling golf equipment, shoes, and gloves. I took the catalogs home, so I knew the different styles of shoes, the leather in the gloves, and the difference between the variety golf balls. I wanted to make Dad proud, and it was fun being so young and impressing the golfers. I took my Dad's pride in being the best you can be at whatever you are doing to heart. I wanted to be a knowledgeable resource for my customers. This knowledge builds confidence. Being confident is another part of a winning mindset.

Dad loved working on 1965-1966 Ford Mustangs. Dad would search for a 65 Ford Mustang for each of us kids. My twin brother and I, plus the grandkids, all had similar experiences with Dad working on the cars together in the garage, getting them ready for when we turned 16 years old so that we would have a cool car to drive. It was the time spent together, working together and getting excited when we got our driver's license. Road trips to pick up parts at the Pony Ranch, where we would find the Mustang parts needed. Dad would let us get dirty, mess up, learn, and laugh together. We could talk to Dad about anything, and there was no judgment zone. When we turned 16 and could drive our shiny Mustang to school, we were so proud because we were vested in the process. He taught us work ethics, patience, being present, pride in things, and caring for them. Having pride is so essential to having a healthy mindset.

Going to work with Bernie

I was a daddy's girl, if you couldn't tell by now. I wanted to
go to work with Dad and watch him sell lawn tractors. So
on a few occasions, I would go in for a couple of hours
with Dad, sit there, and watch him talk with customers.

One thing I remember most was he always laughed with them and asked questions to know which tractor was best for their needs. They were like friends until they walked away from his department. If they weren't seriously thinking about a new lawn tractor before they stopped and spoke with Dad, they were interested now! He had a way of explaining how the new tractor could make their current Life easier and how nice their yard would look. Then when he had a lunch break, he would always show me off in the lunchroom to the other salespeople taking their breaks. They would say, "Bernie is this one of the twins?" Dad had a proud look, and I felt very special.

Then I had a marketing assignment from school to complete and thought I could do something about Sears. So I got an appointment with General Manager at Sears in York, and he explained how they prepared for the printed sales flyers and other parts of the job in marketing. Again I felt fortunate to have this opportunity. A few years later, the General Manager was getting ready to sell his car, and Dad told me about the car, and I said I would love to buy it. As soon as the general Manager knew I was interested in his car, it was mine. So because of Dad and his connections and impressive reputation, I could have opportunities that others did not.

Same within real estate, your professionalism and reputation will allow you to go places you never thought possible. When multiple contracts come in on properties, and it is down to the two best offers, a lot of times the agent on the other end of the transaction holds a lot of weight which way the seller will lean, is the other agent knowledgeable, easy to work with, are they known to be trustworthy.

I have seen agents vote into networking groups based on their stellar real estate reputation and sales experience. When it comes to leadership positions available in your brokerage, are you an option?

Is your Mindset helping you open doors or close them?

Use this space to take your notes:

Bernie thinking outside the box, is a Problem Solver

When working at Sears, some customers wanted to trade in their old lawn tractors, but since Sears did not have a program like that, Dad took it upon himself, when possible, to buy the old tractors from the customers so that he wouldn't lose the sale of the new lawn tractor they wanted to buy.   We all remember Dad in the garage fixing up and painting the old tractors and reselling them!   There were times when a customer would order a new lawn tractor and the deliveries got delayed from the Sears warehouse, and customers complained about how high their grass was getting. Dad would take his truck to the Sears warehouse on his own time, have the new lawn tractor loaded, and personally deliver the tractor to the customer's home. Who does that? Bernie did. He was the poster child for going above and beyond for your customers.

He loved surprising the customers and giving them a WOW experience. He did what he thought was right for the customer and still honored his company by closing the sale. Where there is a will, there's a way. He always looked at things with an abundance mindset, not scarcity.

Dad had so many repeat customers who would only deal with Dad. If they came into the store on Dad's day off, they would return when he was available.

As Agents, you aim to have loyal repeat customers as Dad did. What are you doing to win their trust and show them value and how much you care about them and their situation? How are you going above and beyond for them? Dad was a Problem Solver, just like we are in real estate.   What problems do our customers have that you can solve for them? Do you look at things from an abundance mindset? Doing favors for your clients that seem like a lot of time and effort that is unnecessary to make the sale, or do you complain with a scarcity mindset, not wanting to do extras for the clients because you don't think they will buy anyhow? It is just a waste of my time—two different mindsets.

Let's face it we get paid big bucks to be problem solvers for our clients. Agents who are constantly thinking about how I can help my clients and be resourceful for them, rather than what they can do for me, is the difference between repeat business and having advocated for you and just doing transactions and moving on to the next one.

> **"No one cares how much you know until they know how much you care."**
> **- Theodore Roosevelt**

Bernie's ability to keep things confidential.

There was a story where Bernie caught one of the grandkids hooking out of school one day instead of reprimanding them and squealing to the parents. He listened to why the kid was playing hooky and listened with no judgment. In his gentle, supportive way, Bernie talked with them about the path they were starting to go down and how things could be different, and Dad was there 100% behind them if they chose the other way. He helped them see they had choices and gave them options, and they felt like someone believed in them. Human nature, we all long for someone to believe in us. He never told the parents, and the grandchild never played hooky again. Dad was the master at making you feel important and unique; you knew he had your back. When talking with Dad about important or sensitive topics, he kept things confidential and didn't go around telling everyone your business, which allowed you to feel free to open up to him.

Our clients appreciate our confidentiality, and we owe it to them by our agency laws. But I think there are times when we might talk too much about past real estate situations in front of our clients that might make them feel, "Do they complain about me when we are not around" Please be careful what you say and how you say it, so the clients do not have the perception, you are not be trusted to keep their business private and confidential. How would you rate yourself regarding keeping things confidential when someone shared personal and sensitive information with you that was not meant to be shared with others?

Also, how do you feel when roadblocks come up in transactions? Are you listening to understand what your client is going through so you can best help them and address their fears, or do you immediately get frustrated with them for being a pain in the butt because they seem frustrated with what is going wrong in the transaction and it might appear they blame you? The client might already have their children enrolled in the new school district, most of the house possessions are in boxes for the movers, and now you call them to say there might be a problem with closing. Expect an emotional response, best yet if you can deliver the news in person rather than on the phone, and please never send a message like that by text. Once the shock of the issue wears off, you can provide options and comfort the client because you are the problem Solver, represent them in the transaction, and, more importantly, care about them. When real estate is going well, everyone looks good; it is the times when things go wrong that the strong and resourceful agents stand out!

Consider how you react when presented with bad news on a transaction and how you deliver that news to your client.

Bernie knew how important fun was in your day.

I remember coming home from my first job working at a golf course one night, and I was so excited about the money I made that day. Dad said Dolly, remember to have fun. I was so driven at the golf course, working weekends and holidays and trying to get a following of clientele when I worked the bartender shift that I didn't go out with other kids my age that I knew from school and have fun! Dad was a big fan of enjoying what you do, surrounding yourself with good people, and having fun. I made my job fun, so when I worked the bar shift, I would think about what fun drinks I could make as a special for Ladies' Day golf. When the buses of golfers would come in from Maryland to play our golf course, how can I get them to enjoy coming to the bar after their round of golf? Instead of hanging outside in the pavilion area. So, I learned what they enjoyed drinking and ensured we had plenty of it. I knew their names and called them by name when they came in and had their drinks ready.   I had so much fun with this group from Maryland, and they could tell how much I enjoyed them, so they kept coming back!

Have fun with your real estate career. Join groups that enjoy the same hobbies as you do. If you drop off little pop-bys (gifts to past clients, usually $5 or less), do it in a convertible or go with someone fun and make your day enjoyable. Have coffee or lunch dates with clients. The more fun you have with Life, the more positive things will happen to you.

Dad loved his 49 Ford Pickup that he worked on to make it look sharp, and the color scheme was the same as the brown and tan truck he drove to work. Fun Memories shared by friends and family who watched and helped Dad refurbish this truck will be cherished forever. I admired his dedication and detail in trying to make everything come out just right, especially the wood bed of the truck that had a lot of shellac on it, and it shined!

Giving to others

The best way to feel good is to do something nice for someone else or give to charity.

Dad loved to take produce from the garden into Sears and mark 75 cents on a bag of 13 ears of corn from his garden. Dad would walk through the garden in the morning, pulling the corn and putting it in bags to take to his coworkers. Dad just beamed at being able to do that. My twin brother said the other night he saw a dozen ears of corn was $9.00 at the country store. Wow, how times have changed.

When Dad would plow the snow for all the neighbors, it made him feel as good as the neighbors who didn't have to go out in the cold to plow and shovel.

The golf course I worked at had bartender events to raise charity money. One year was for Muscular Dystrophy, and the following year was for Multiple Sclerosis. I loved how all my coworkers and golfers got into helping me raise money and donate to these great causes. I was hooked on the joy everyone shared. It was such a wonderful feeling to help the less fortunate, and the camaraderie felt with others while doing the activities to raise money.

Budweiser

Then I got involved with the community service committee at the Realtors Association of York and Adams counties. This committee provided money and services to homeless shelters, domestic abuse shelters, Habitat for Humanity, and anything to do with housing needs.   It was so rewarding to see the work that the volunteers did and, once again, how people pulled together. One evening we hosted a Halloween party for the children who happened to be in the domestic abuse shelter with their mothers, and we were trying to bring an evening of some "normal" for them and fun. We provided games, costumes, food, decorations, and candy.   That evening, it seemed like they had forgotten about their situation and were just kids, even for a few hours. They were so grateful.

My current real estate company supports the Sunshine Kids, which is a charity to provide children battling cancer the funds to send them on a trip with a nurse, so they can be with other children who look like them, with no hair, missing limbs, and be normal kids for a week. When I met the children, I was impressed with their attitudes. When I walked into the room, there was a high level of energy, laughter, gratitude, and appreciation for the day. I learned so much from the Sunshine Kids. They understood that Life is to be lived with passion and joy every day because tomorrow is not guaranteed. Many children who grew up and beat their cancer went on to go into careers of helping or entertaining others, bringing joy.

Through talking with family and friends, there were a few things that kept coming up; Dad never told you what you should do, he would pull you aside, and he would say stuff like, "Well, now let's look at this a minute, maybe there is another way to approach this, help you see options in situations. He had a way of letting you make an educated decision without feeling like you were being reprimanded or told what to do. His advice came from a place of wisdom, and people respected him. He also listened to what you had to say and was genuinely interested in YOU. If we learn from that as salespeople to help our clients with options and ideas while trying to make huge decisions and make them feel heard and understood, they will trust our advice and be loyal clients for years. Another thing I heard over and over was he was a gentleman who always wanted to do the right thing and was willing to help anyone and always happy!

Summary of Bernie's Art Of Communication

Do unto others as you would like to be treated!

A smile, manners, listening to people, making people feel good around you, and being present with someone are essential to communication. How would you rate yourself as a great communicator? 1 to 10?

Do people see you as trustworthy?

Do you see things from an abundance mindset or a scarcity perspective?

What can you do to be more resourceful in solving problems for our clients?

Let's all try communicating better, less by text and more by talking to one another!

How do you put fun into your day?

When did you do something nice for someone, expecting nothing? How did you feel?

Bernie was the master of communication. He left people feeling heard, loved, special, and inspired.

Use this space to take your notes:

Chapter 6 - Bernie's Law of Attraction

Growing up, I didn't ever hear of the Law of Attraction but was blessed to live it while watching Dad.

> **"Where Focus Goes Energy Flows"**
> **- Tony Robbins**

Your thoughts are like a magnet to what you attract into your Life. I remember Dad's excitement when I told him I was hired at the local golf course at age 15. My math teacher, who happened to be the golf coach for my high school, approached me about the job opening at the local golf club, and he recommended me. He said the golf course needed someone with a cheerful personality to work the counter in the pro shop. I was attracted to that job because of my outlook, and I was always happy, just like my Dad. My Dad said this job was an excellent opportunity to be surrounded by the people that Dad felt had careers, owned businesses, and overall had a better outlook on Life. Plus, I would be in a fun environment. He was thrilled with the potential of the new friends I would make.

Little did I know that eight years later, as I was working the bartender shift, someone would walk in that had worked with my Dad previously at Sears but now was a real estate broker. I wanted more for myself at this point and was interested in sales. I was 23 years old and had already bought my first home and was intrigued by that process and thought a real estate career might be for me. So when the real estate broker that had previously known my Dad showed up at my bar that day, I couldn't help but feel like that was no accident. When I told him I was considering getting into real estate, he immediately called his office, and I had an appointment with the trainer that week. My real estate journey started that day.

Your positive Mindset opens up so many opportunities for you. It is essential in building the Legacy you want to leave behind, whether it is how you treat people, your wealth, your business, investment properties, or charities you started. No one wants to be around Debbie Downers.

What kind of clients are you attracting? What kind of experience are you attracting while at work?

If you hold a thought for 17 seconds, the Law of Attraction brings you what you think about, whether it is good or bad. Self-talk is so important to be aware of what you are telling yourself. Example: I never win anything, I am a terrible golfer, I cannot lose weight, I hate to exercise. Well, guess what? Your subconscious mind will ensure that obstacles get in your way so you can't succeed. Instead, how about I feel lucky today? I will have the best round of golf today that I have ever had. I am getting leaner and more fit every day. I love walking in the fresh air. I am going to meet someone today that needs help with Real Estate. Watch the difference in your attitude; your subconscious mind finds everything to help you succeed. Suddenly someone at work is looking for a walking buddy over lunch; at Starbucks, the car in front of you paid for your coffee. You get a call from someone that has been thinking of selling their home. I write in my journal, "Everything is always working out for me" I even have a tee shirt with that saying on it. Believe it! When setting your Goals, Your Conscious Mind (the captain) is the one that hears your goal of losing 30 pounds. Your subconscious mind (the sailor who obeys the orders) listens to what you are thinking; who am I kidding? I will not be able to lose that weight; the holidays are coming. So, the subconscious mind works on providing obstacles to your goal. But imagine if you believed you would lose weight and how different things would be when your subconscious mind is in harmony with your goals! During the day, you must pivot or change the "radio station," as Abraham Hicks calls it. If you are in a negative situation, maybe a real estate deal just blew up, your thoughts are going off the rails, this is where your awareness of the problem comes in, and you make a conscious effort to switch the "radio station." Rather than walk down the hall and tell three more Realtors about your doom and gloom. Take a break, take a quick walk outside, and drink water. Break the patterns of what the old you would have done. Pivot to the thinking of resolution to the situation, how can we prevent this from happening again.

How can I help these folks get housing?

How can I help others from what I learned in this transaction?

Did you ever notice that negative people have a lot of problems?

Did you ever notice that positive people seem to have all the luck and things are always working out for them?

Use this space to take your notes:

Summary of Bernies Law of Attraction

Bernie attracted loyal customers, wonderful friends and family, and people that would do anything for him. Because that is Who He was.

Your thoughts are magical and so powerful. The Life you are currently living is the direct result of your thoughts and beliefs. How cool is it that you control your Life through your thoughts and beliefs?   If you don't like what you see, change your thoughts. Where Focus Goes Energy Flows!

Self-talk can either lift you or drag you down. Be kind to yourself. There is only one YOU.

Do you truly believe in yourself and what you want?

Doing this will motivate you to continue your growth journey!

As Bernie would say, "You can do anything you set your mind to, kid."

I believe in you too!

Chapter 7 Being a Leader

Bernie took Initiative.

What it means to take initiative is you do things without having to be told; you find out what you need to know; you keep going when things get tough; and you spot and take advantage of opportunities that others pass by.

I was reading about people with initiative, and they are motivated to do things. If you take initiative, means you are willing to get things done on your own, which can be risky because there is no one else to blame if things go wrong.

Examples of Initiative skills are; Confidence, Self-Management, Decisiveness, Problem-Solving, Professionalism, Conflict-resolution and Adaptability. I thought wow, that describes Bernie.

Growing up I never thought about dad as a "leader". Now looking back, I see how everyone loved being near him, we followed him and his advice, he was wise and calm when things got crazy. He influenced us to want to be better and do better. He lead by example. He took initiative at home to get things done. He was always the first one outside in the morning. At Sears he took initiative to know all the new features and conveniences the new model lawn tractors could provide his customers. You could always find Bernie on a mission to find just the right Mustang vehicle to buy to work on with his grandchildren.

Initiative can be as simple as someone emptying the Dishwasher without being told, haha!

When I think of the successful Agents, they all have initiative. They are not afraid to try new things, they do not need someone to remind them to get to work. When Problems come up, they get to work solving them. Not spend their time blaming others. Successful Agents are great at brainstorming and looking for opportunities to take advantage of rather than waiting for someone to hand them something.

I hear agents say all the time, I want more leads given to me. Leaders and agents with initiative look for ways to create more leads to grow their business. They take responsibility for themselves.

Great Intentions do not mean anything until you take action. "We Judge Ourselves By Our Intentions, Others Judge Us By Our Actions" Brian Buffini

Bernie was a person of Influence.

If your actions inspire others to dream more, learn more, do more and become more, you are a Leader.

Bernie was always inspiring us to be what we wanted to be. He praised us and was present with us on our journeys. He always seemed to give us just the right amount of freedom to do our thing, but always there to be the caring parent to help us from making big mistakes.

Agents influence their clients by reminding them of their visions and goals. The buyer who wants to buy that house because it is close to the schools and the kids will love the park, and help the buyer not get hung up on the rise of mortgage interest rate. Or the Seller who wants to move to be closer to their grandchildren in a different state and keeps them focused on the grandchildren instead of a repair needed to the home to close the sale.

> **"If you help enough people get what they want, you will get what you want"**
>
> **- Zig Ziglar**

Team Leaders inspire and motivate their agents to go out and educate and serve the clients to help them get what they want, which also grows the agents and the team.

A Football coach, Pastor, Teacher, Real Estate Agent, Parents are all examples of Leaders. Every day we have opportunities to lift people up or tear them down, the choice is yours.

Attitude influences people.

How do people feel when they leave you?

Was your attitude one of kindness, understanding, positivity, curiosity.

Use this space to take your notes:

Bernie had Intuition

Intuition is the ability to understand something immediately, without the need for conscious reasoning. Go with your gut feeling.

Bernie could sense when as kids we needed to talk about something important, or as a salesperson he decided on the spot to buy someone's used tractor so they could afford to buy the new Sears tractor. His gut told him it was the thing to do for the customer and he would be fine reselling the used tractor.   He was right!

Agents use their intuition when working with clients in helping them make decisions, you might sense that the parents need to see the house to give the blessing for the kids to feel comfortable about moving forward with the deal. Agents use their intuition/ gut feeling in safety situations when showing vacant properties.   Marketing is another way Agents use their intuition for what is right for them.

The power of Intuition in Leadership Decision-Making:

Speed - Leaders often need to make rapid decisions. Intuition can help cut through the noise and provide an immediate sense of direction.

Creativity - Intuition can spark innovative ideas that may not surface through conventional brainstorming or analytical process. Trust your gut.

Empathy - Intuitive leaders are often more attuned to the emotions and needs of their team, children, students, and agents. This empathy fosters a more positive environment to work and play.

Risk Assessment - An intuitive leader may have a better sense of when to take risks or when to avoid unnecessary pitfalls.

Intuition versus Rationality - It is crucial to balance trusting your gut and relying on a rational analysis. When your gut is telling you something, take a moment to reflect on the source of this feeling. Is it based on past experiences or merely a reaction to fear and anxiety?

Lead from Within - embrace your gift of intuition and allow it to lead you to uncharted waters and find creativity and innovation.

Why? Because greatness lies within you!

Conclusion

At the opening of this, book we spoke of two types of readers.
The one who will make excuses not to act on any of the ideas presented in this book.
The other reader will be open-minded and ready to start closer relationships, financial success, health and well-being.

Which reader are you?
The choice is yours!

I hope you took pause at the end of the chapters to answer the questions and if you haven't yet answered, now is your time to take action.

Go back and dig in.
Get your MINDSET clear and begin your transformation!

Now that you are ready to move forward, Let's set course.
What are the 3 top goals you set for yourself.

1. ____

____

____

____

2. ____

____

____

____

3. ____

____

____

____

How will things be different after you have reached your goals and are living the Bernie Mindset?

____

____

____

____

How will YOU be different after you have reached your goals and are living the Bernie Mindset?

____

____

____

____

Visualize it daily "as if" it is done, and it will be so.

____

____

____

____

____

> **"The things you do for yourself are gone when you are gone, but the things you do for others remain as your legacy"**
>
> -   **Kalu Ndukewe Kalu**

What will your Legacy be?

To be Legendary is to be admired.

Become a Legendary (admired) Real Estate Agent with a Legendary (admired) Mindset!

Living Life like Bernie!

Thank you!

Thank you for being on this journey with me. I must admit
I felt vulnerable at times, but I was comforted thinking that
someone will take this information to help them enjoy a
better life.

A heartfelt thank you to my loving husband of 36 years for
being my best friend and biggest supporter of whatever I
want to do. My nieces and nephews, family, and friends,
for the pure joy you bring to my life.

Big thank you to my Coach
Kim Johnson for pushing me
WAY beyond my comfort zone and helping me with writing
this book. I could not have done this without you.

9 798861 451208